# Scales & Arpeggios
# Piano

### Grade 2

Good legato, even fingers, firm tone and a musical curve are the essential features for playing scales and arpeggios well.

The suggested fingering shown here is not obligatory; any practical and systematic fingering which produces a good result will be accepted in the examination. Some alternative fingering is shown as follows: 4/3. In the playing of arpeggios, the decision as to which fingering to adopt will depend on the size and shape of the player's hand. Examiners do not comment on the choice of fingering unless it interferes with an even, legato flow.

In the examination, all scales and arpeggios must be played from memory.

Metronome marks shown here indicate *minimum* recommended speeds for the examination.

Reference must always be made to the syllabus for the year in which the examination is to be taken, in case any changes have been made to the requirements.

The Associated Board of the Royal Schools of Music

© 1994 by The Associated Board of the Royal Schools of Music

Sharps #
Father
Charles
Goes
Down
And
Ends
Battle

Flats ♭
B
E
A
D
G
C
F

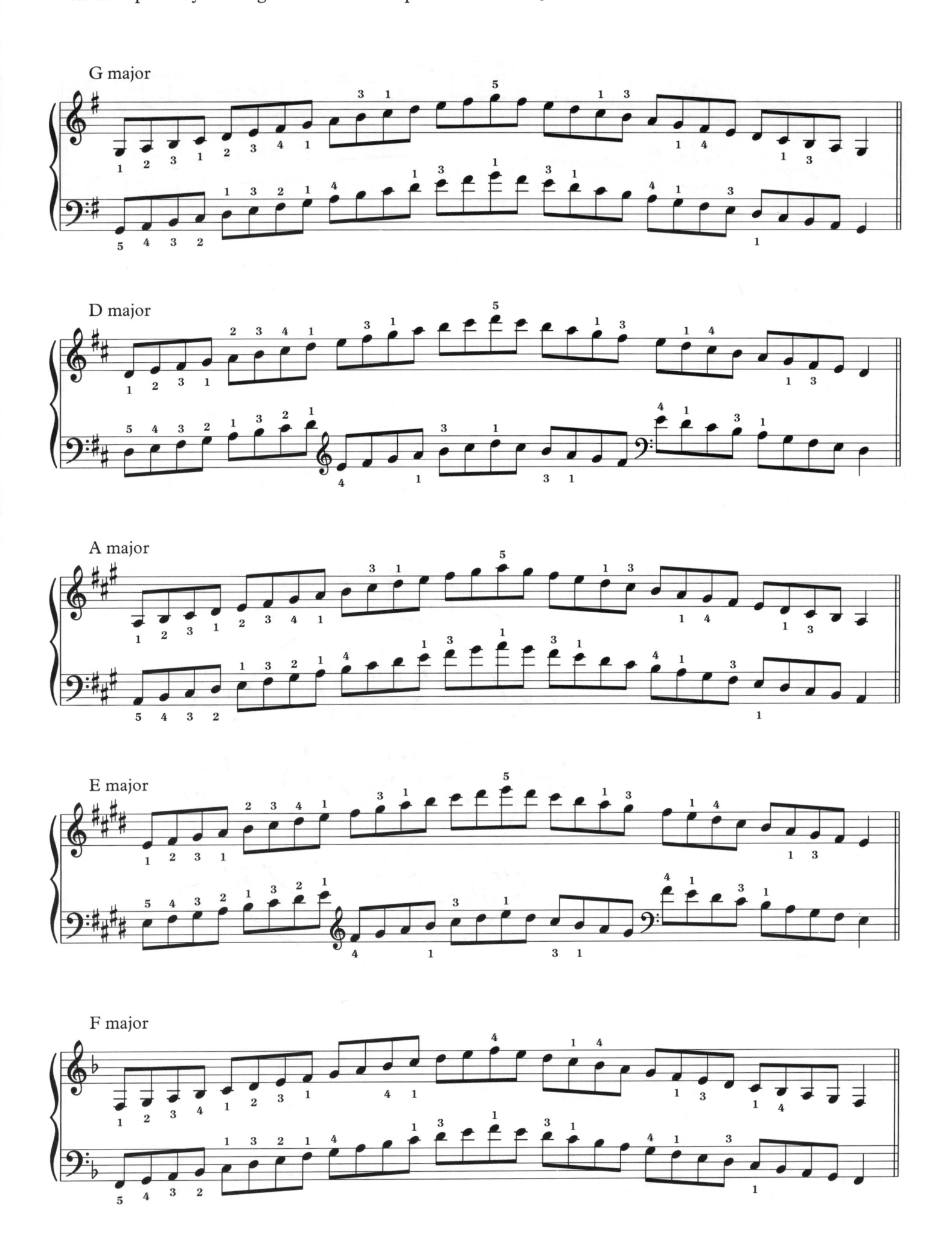

**Major Scales** in similar motion
Hands separately and together an octave apart: 2 octaves: ♩ = 66

G major

D major

A major

E major

F major

**Minor Scales** (melodic *or* harmonic at candidate's choice) in similar motion
Hands separately and together an octave apart: 2 octaves: ♩ = 66

E minor melodic

B minor melodic

D minor melodic

or

E minor harmonic    *(handwritten: F SHARP & D SHARP)*

B minor harmonic    *(handwritten: F, C & A SHARP)*

D minor harmonic    *(handwritten: B NAT & C SHARP)*

**Major Scales** in contrary motion

Hands together beginning and ending on the key-note (unison): 2 octaves: ♩ = 66

C major

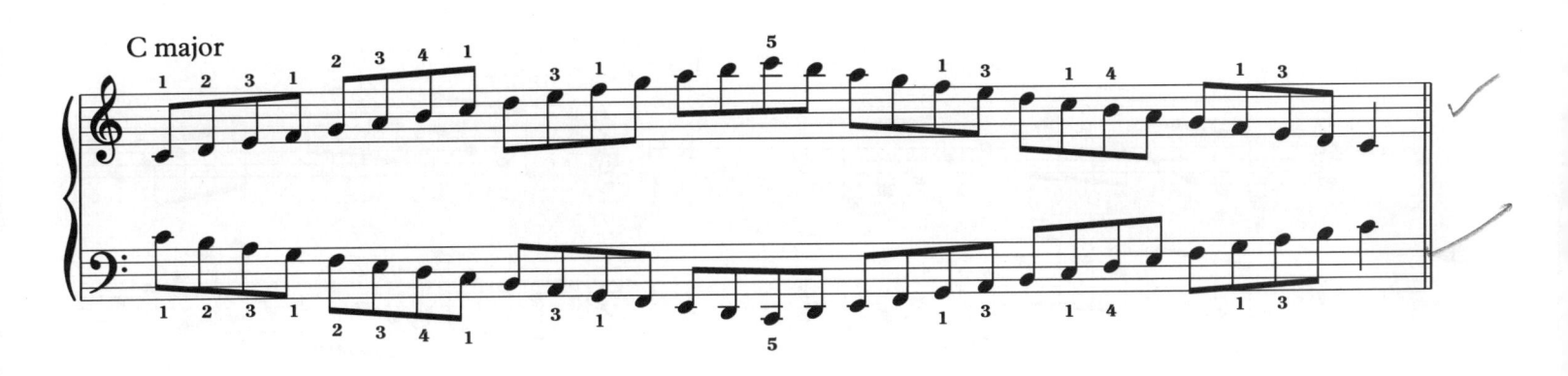

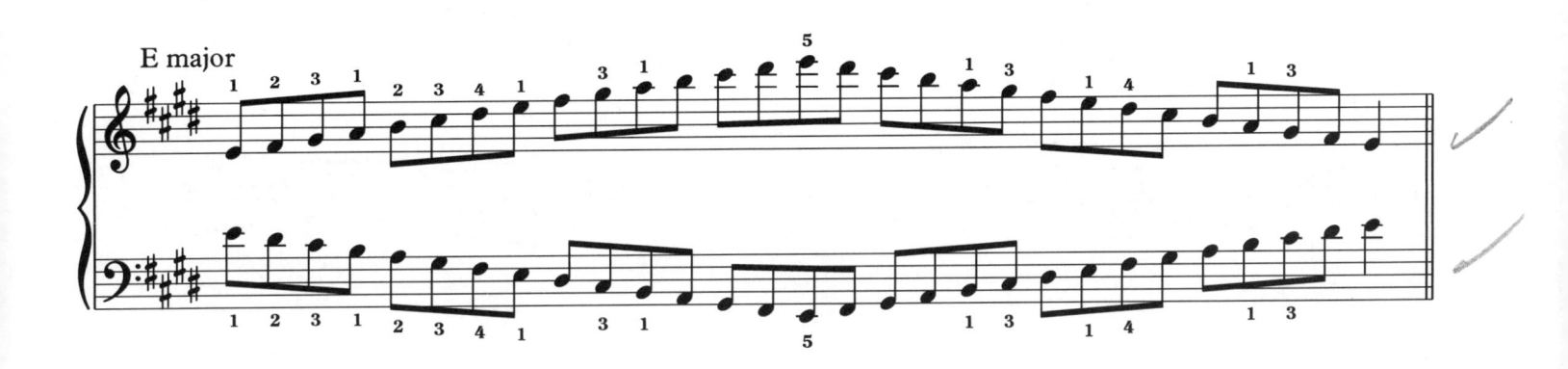

E major

**Chromatic Scale**

Hands separately: 1 octave: ♩ = 66

Beginning on D

R.H.

L.H.

**Arpeggios** of major and minor common chords in root position
Hands separately: 2 octaves: ♩ = 63

G major

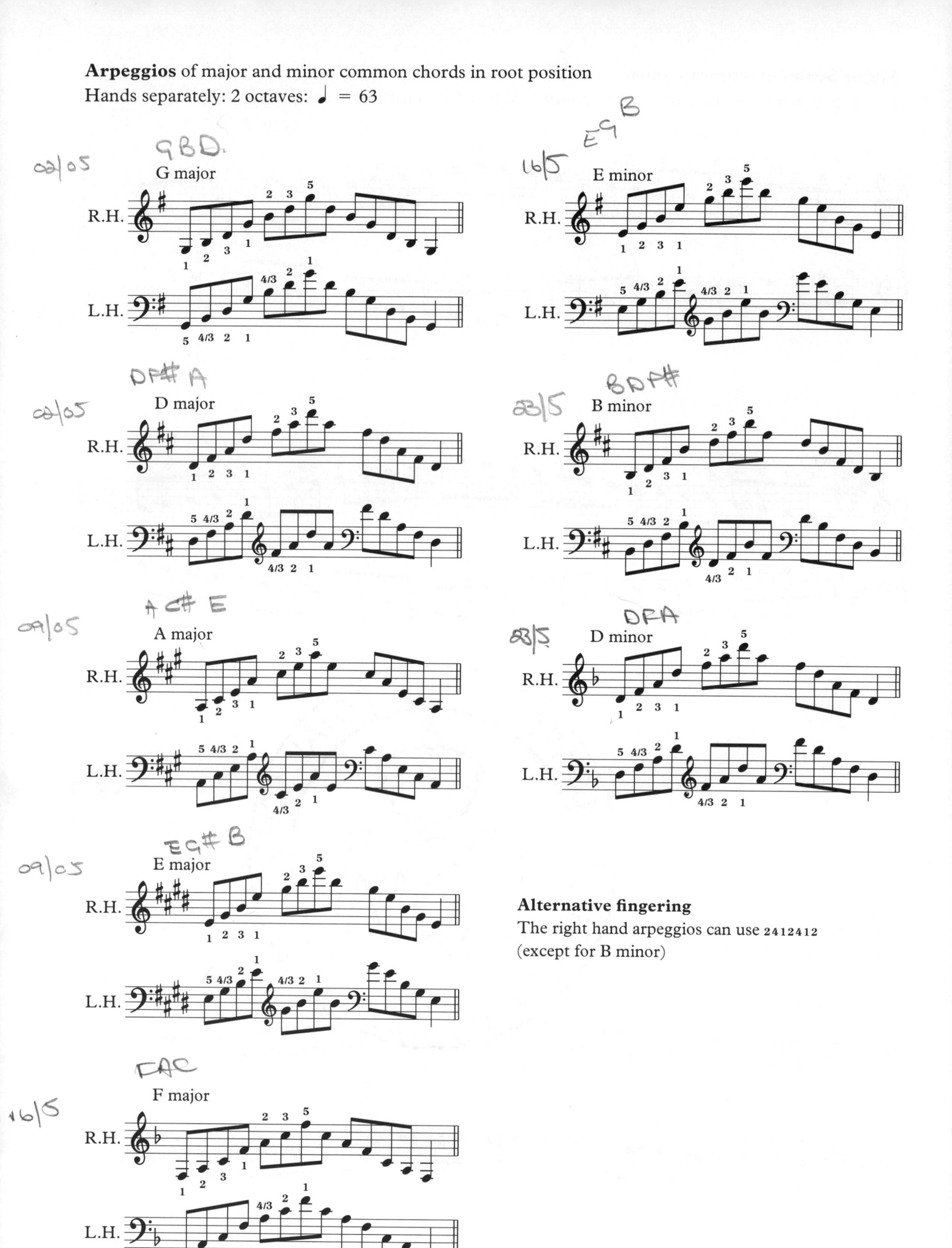

E minor

D major

B minor

A major

D minor

**Alternative fingering**

The right hand arpeggios can use 2 4 1 2 4 1 2
(except for B minor)

E major

F major